SHARKS

Printed in Singapore

95   96   97   98   99   5   4   3   2

Library of Congress Cataloging-in-Publication Data

Perrine, Doug.
    Sharks / Doug Perrine.
        p.   cm.
    ISBN 0-89658-270-1
    I. Sharks   I. Title
QL638.9.P435 1995
597'.31–dc20   94–42427
                                                         CIP

Distributed in Canada by Raincoast Books,
8680 Cambie Street, Vancouver, B. C. V6P 6M9, Canada

Published by Voyageur Press, Inc.
P. O. Box 338, 123 North Second Street, Stillwater, MN 55082 U.S.A.
612-430-2210, fax 612-430-2211

Please write or call, or stop by, for our free catalog of natural history publications. Our toll-free number to place an order or to obtain a free
catalog is 800-888-WOLF (800-888-9653)

Educators, fundraisers, premium and gift buyers, publicists and marketing managers: Looking for creative products and new sales ideas?
Voyageur Press books are available at special discounts when purchased in quantities, and special editions can be created to your
specifications. For details contact the marketing manager.

Photographs © 1995:

Front Cover © David Fleetham (Innerspace Visions)
Back Cover © David Fleetham (Innerspace Visions)
Page 1 © Doug Perrine (Innerspace Visions)
Page 4 © Doug Perrine (Innerspace Visions)
Page 6 © David Fleetham (Innerspace Visions)
Page 9 © Doug Perrine (Innerspace Visions)
Page 10 © Doug Perrine (Innerspace Visions)
Page 11 © David Fleetham (Innerspace Visions)
Page 12 Top Left © Mark Conlin (Innerspace Visions)
Page 12 Top Right © Scott Michael (Innerspace Visions)
Page 12 Bottom Left © Norbert Wu (Innerspace Visions)
Page 12 Bottom Right © Doug Perrine (Innerspace Visions)
Page 13 © Doug Perrine (Innerspace Visions)
Page 15 © Doug Perrine (Innerspace Visions)
Page 16 Top © Dr Samuel Gruber (Innerspace Visions)
Page 16 Bottom © Mark Conlin (Innerspace Visions)
Page 19 © Mark Strickland (Innerspace Visions)
Page 21 © Doug Perrine (Innerspace Visions)
Page 22 © Doug Perrine (Innerspace Visions)

Page 24 © Doug Perrine (Innerspace Visions)
Page 25 © Michael Nolan (Innerspace Visions)
Page 26 © Jeff Rotman (Innerspace Visions)
Page 27 © Doug Perrine (Innerspace Visions)
Page 29 © Doug Perrine (Innerspace Visions)
Page 30 © Doug Perrine (Innerspace Visions)
Page 32 © Doug Perrine (Innerspace Visions)
Page 33 Top Left © Mark Conlin (Innerspace Visions)
Page 33 Top Right © Mark Conlin (Innerspace Visions)
Page 33 Bottom Left © Mark Conlin (Innerspace Visions)
Page 33 Bottom Right © Mark Conlin (Innerspace Visions)
Page 34 © David Fleetham (Innerspace Visions)
Page 37 © Bruce Rasner (Innerspace Visions)
Page 38 © Doug Perrine (Innerspace Visions)
Page 40 © Mark Conlin (Innerspace Visions)
Page 41 © Doug Perrine (Innerspace Visions)
Page 43 © Mark Conlin (Innerspace Visions)
Page 44 © Mark Strickland (Innerspace Visions)
Page 47 © Doug Perrine (Innerspace Visions)

Page 48 © Doug Perrine (Innerspace Visions)
Page 49 © Doug Perrine (Innerspace Visions)
Page 50 © Doug Perrine (Innerspace Visions)
Page 53 © Tom Campbell (Innerspace Visions)
Page 54 © James D. Watt (Innerspace Visions)
Page 55 © Doug Perrine (Innerspace Visions)
Page 56 © James D. Watt (Innerspace Visions)
Page 58 © Chris Huss (Innerspace Visions)
Page 60 © Bruce Rasner (Innerspace Visions)
Page 61 © Doug Perrine (Innerspace Visions)
Page 62 © Howard Hall (Innerspace Visions)
Page 65 Top © David Fleetham (Innerspace Visions)
Page 65 Bottom Left © Andrea and Antonella Ferrari
(Innerspace Visions)
Page 65 Bottom Right © Doug Perrine (Innerspace Visions)
Page 66 © Doug Perrine (Innerspace Visions)
Page 67 © Doug Perrine (Innerspace Visions)
Page 68 © Doug Perrine (Innerspace Visions)
Page 71 © Doug Perrine (Innerspace Visions)

SHARKS

Doug Perrine

Voyageur Press

Contents

Misunderstood 'Monsters'

The shark didn't turn and try to bite me, or even flinch, as I was expecting. Instead it seemed to relax. It felt nothing like I had expected. It was soft, smooth, and slippery — not rough like sandpaper. But I was feeling the inside of the shark and at that moment I began to wonder what I was doing there, sitting on the ocean floor with one arm up to its elbow inside the birth canal of a three meter (10ft) long pregnant lemon shark — a variety with many sharp teeth, often listed in books as 'dangerous'.

I was in the Bahamas on a research cruise with scientists who were studying the hormonal systems of this species. Important information could be gathered from this shark on the hormonal changes that take place during pregnancy. In order to take the blood and urine samples needed, they had to catch some sharks. The chief scientist, Dr Samuel H Gruber of the University of Miami, was concerned that her pups could be harmed if the shark struggled while the samples were being taken. Also, he was interested in discovering how many pups there were and the ratio of males to females. The mother was captured on her way from the deep reef, where the adults live, into the lagoon where the pups are born, so we knew that she was ready to give birth. Dr Gruber's assistant, Bob Jureit, released the pups underwater before the mother was brought up to the research boat to have the samples drawn. After twelve little sharks had been pulled out he could still feel the tail of one more inside, but he couldn't reach it. He needed someone with smaller hands to reach all the way in for the last shark. Suddenly all eyes focused on me.

I grabbed the tail of a shark pup and began to pull. I got it almost half way out but it slipped out of my fingers and wriggled back into the womb. For nearly a year, a thin membrane had protected the embryo until it had grown into a 60cm (2ft) long miniature version of its mother. Now fully developed, it was capable of living entirely on its own, needing no further help from its mother. Finally, I managed to tug the baby shark out of its mother. It turned and swam quickly away, snapping the umbilical cord which had passed nourishment to it. Among the roots of the mangrove trees in the lagoon it would find safety from the many predators that might try to eat it, including its own mother. After the samples were drawn the mother too was released, and swam slowly back out towards deep water.

Thirteen is a typical litter size for the lemon shark, and about average for the requiem shark family (Carcharhinidae). This group includes most of the common sharks seen in shallow waters. The name 'requiem' may be derived from the French word for shark, *requin*, or it may come from the Catholic mass for the dead, a likely association, as most people think of sharks as 'primitive man-eaters'. Feeling the baby shark squirming inside its mother made me realize that these animals are not the 'primitive beasts' usually portrayed by the media. Live birth is an advanced evolutionary characteristic and sharks are among the few animals on earth, apart from mammals, which do this. Fish, birds, amphibians, reptiles, and invertebrates all normally reproduce by releasing eggs. Sharks display many other advanced characteristics, including large brains. In laboratory tests of learning ability, sharks performed about as well as most small mammals.

Sharks rarely offer any threat to human beings. We had to be very careful with the lemon sharks that we worked with because they are prone to bite in self-defense when being handled. However, if left alone to mind their own business, they avoided humans whenever they could. Their long sharp teeth may look scary, but are actually perfectly adapted for seizing the small fish and octopus that make up most of their diet.

When I first learned to scuba dive in the early 1970s, I believed, like most people at the time, that if a shark saw you in the water, you were as good as dead. On my second scuba dive in the ocean, I swam around a coral head and came face to face with a small blacktip reef shark. Terrified, I bolted in the opposite direction. Looking over my shoulder to see if the fearsome beast was gaining on me, I saw the shark

A newborn lemon shark swims
away from its mother, with the umbilical cord and
placenta still attached. Striped sharksuckers sometimes
assist with births by biting off the umbilical cord and
eating the afterbirth.

fleeing in the opposite direction. Obviously the shark felt that it had more to fear from people than the other way around. As it turned out, the shark was right.

When people find out that I spend a good portion of my time photographing sharks, the first question they nearly always ask is, 'Have you ever been bitten?' I'm embarrassed to admit that the answer is yes. Embarrassed because it was my own fault. Any large animal, domestic or wild, is potentially dangerous. The accident happened on a dive trip after one of the crew told me that there was a shark behind the boat. I was foolish enough to grab my camera and jump into the water without asking more questions or observing the shark's behavior. I only learned after I came back out of the water that my shipmates had been teasing it with a stringer of freshly-speared fish, dropping the fish into the water and then pulling them back out just as the shark charged. By the time I found this out, I had spent the most terrifying few minutes of my life defending myself with my camera as the shark circled closer and closer, snapping at my exposed arms. The encounter ended when I slammed the camera into the shark's mouth and sustained a gash that required eight stitches to close as I pulled my hand back out of the open jaws.

Silvertip Shark

The shark that bit me was a Caribbean reef shark, a species considered dangerous because it sometimes attacks spear-fishermen when competing for their catch. However, the shark which is responsible for most shark bites is the nurse shark. This

The whitetip reef shark, a ubiquitous species in the tropical Pacific and Indian Oceans, hunts for its food among the nooks and crannies of the coral reef. By day it is often found sleeping in a cave or under a ledge. It poses little or no threat to divers and swimmers.

Horn Shark
Zebra Horn Shark

Chain Dogfish
Spotted Wobbegong Shark

species is usually considered harmless because it feeds on bottom-dwelling shellfish, mostly at night, and spends most of the day sleeping with its head under a ledge or coral head. Many divers can't resist the urge to pull this shark's tail when they see it sticking out of a cave, although the result seems quite predictable. Most injuries from sharks should be called 'shark defenses', rather than 'shark attacks', because the shark is defending itself against a provocation by a human.

Other 'shark attacks' occur when sharks and other sea creatures begin to scavenge the body of a person who has drowned or died of other causes. In most cases, an autopsy is not conducted. Because of the presence of shark bites on the body, the death is then listed in shark attack files which show that, worldwide, there are around 50-75 unprovoked shark attacks per year, 10-15 of which are fatal. Many other animals, including dogs, pigs,

Caribbean Reef Shark.

and deer, kill more people than this each year. Statistically, the most deadly creature in the world (apart from humans), is the common honey bee.

Many books and articles about sharks continually refer to 'the shark', suggesting all sharks behave the same. A class is a very large grouping of animals and sharks and rays comprise the class Chondrichthyes. Another example of a class is Mammalia. To talk about 'the shark' is equivalent to making a statement about 'the mammal', implying that it is equally true of whales and rats. Apart from the nearly 500 species of skates and rays which are not biologically distinct from sharks, only differently shaped, there are about 375-475 species of sharks. This number is approximate because there are species which have not yet been cataloged, and certainly species which have not yet been discovered. Also, scientists do not agree entirely on which sharks should be classified as separate species, and which may be lumped together as a single species.

Between three and five new species of shark are discovered each year. Among all these different types of sharks, there is tremendous diversity. The whale shark is the largest fish in the ocean, while the pygmy shark grows to no more than 27cm (11in). Some sharks live at the surface of the ocean; others in its deepest depths. Some swim constantly; others lie on the bottom. Some sharks feed on plankton that they strain out of the water; others bite off large chunks of fish, turtles, and marine mammals.

In spite of this tremendous variety of diets, there is no shark species which includes humans among the regular items on its diet. The vast majority are harmless to humans and only a handful can be considered dangerous. Even among these, most attacks are not feeding attacks, but bites or slashes which do not remove flesh. Many of these may be defensive or territorial, resulting from a diver encroaching upon a shark's 'personal space'. Even in cases where part or all of the victim is consumed, it is believed that the majority of attacks are the result of mistaken identity. A frequently cited example is the resemblance, when seen from below, of a surfer on a short board to a sea lion. The reason why sharks should have little interest in consuming humans is obvious: there were no people in the ocean when their feeding habits evolved.

Today, more and more divers have become fascinated by these beautifully adapted animals. Recent studies reveal that many species which were once considered extremely dangerous, such as sand tigers ('grey nurses'), are in fact completely inoffensive. Now when I find myself surrounded by hundreds of hammerhead sharks (listed in some books as 'man-eaters'), my only fear is that the noise of my exhalations will scare away these timid creatures.

The massive mouth of the whale shark is not used for swallowing divers, but rather for engulfing shoals of plankton and small schooling fish.

The demand for shark fins poses a serious threat for sharks. Despite this, many thousands are slaughtered in sporting tournaments every year, where no part of the shark is utilized.

Predators in Peril

Sharks have a great deal to fear from humans. Compared to the 10-15 people killed by sharks each year, over 100 million sharks perish at the hands of humans annually and many populations may face extinction. Sharks are killed for many reasons, including fear, food, sport, and 'machismo', but the great majority perish due to simple greed. Many shark products have commercial value, including: the flesh; the skin for high-quality leather; teeth and jaws for ornaments; liver oil for cosmetics, medicines, vitamin A, and skin-care products; and cartilage for false cancer 'cures'. However, the product that drives the market are the fins. After drying, collagen fibers are extracted from them, cleaned, and processed to make 'shark fin soup'. In spite of the fact that these fibers have little flavor or nutritional value, the soup is considered a delicacy, and may sell in the Orient for more than $100 (£65) a bowl.

Over the years, shark fisheries have come and gone. In the early part of the century, sponge fishermen in Florida killed sharks to boil them down for their oil. The oil was then thrown on the ocean to smooth the surface of the water and make it easier to see the sponges from the boat. That ended when a plague killed off the sponges. In the 1940s to 1950s a number of shark fisheries sprang up to supply the market for vitamin A. That ended with the discovery of a method for its synthetic production. However, most shark fisheries, such as the one for dogfish sharks to supply the 'fish and chips' market in the UK, have ended only when the number of sharks dropped too low for the fishery to be sustained.

The explosive growth of the Chinese economy and rapid expansion of trade with the outside world during the 1980s and 1990s created an unprecedented situation. Suddenly there was an insatiable demand for shark fins of almost any size or type. Improvements in shipbuilding and navigational electronics meant that shark fishing boats could now go anywhere in the world, moving from one place to another as local shark populations were destroyed. The fins are now so much more valuable than the rest of the shark that the carcass is often discarded after the fins are removed, to save storage space on the boat. Often the fins are sliced off when the shark is still alive and the mutilated shark is dumped back into the water to die a slow and agonizing death.

Why should we be concerned about this situation? After all, wouldn't the ocean be much safer without sharks? The answer is no. The chance of being attacked by a shark is already less than the chance of being struck by lightning. The real dangers for people in the water are drowning, exposure, and being struck by a boat. In the USA, for example, drowning incidents outnumber shark attacks by 1,000 to 1. Without sharks, the whole experience of being in a natural ocean wilderness would be immeasurably reduced. It would be like being on the Serengeti with no lions or cheetahs. In losing the opportunity to view these magnificent and superbly-adapted predators in the wild, we are also losing part of our spiritual connection with nature.

But something else would be changed as well – the whole ecology of the ocean. Predators control the populations of their prey species in a beneficial way. They eliminate diseased and genetically defective individuals, and they stabilize population fluctuations. On land, when we have removed the natural predators of deer, for example, their populations have exploded until they overgrazed their food supply and died of starvation and disease. In the ocean we are not sure what all the consequences of removing the apex predators from the food pyramid might be. We do have one example, though. A shark fishery in Tasmania collapsed after two years of overfishing. Shortly afterwards, the fishery for spiny lobsters also collapsed and fishermen observed a lot of octopus in the area. Octopuses are both major predators of spiny lobster and an important food item for sharks. It seems that once the numbers of octopus were no longer controlled by the sharks, they became too numerous and decimated the lobsters. Economically, for those other than shark fishermen, it doesn't make sense to allow sharks to be fished out, not only because of the possible damage to more

*This whitetip reef shark was caught within the Similan Islands National
Park of Thailand, a 'protected' area for sharks. In most shark fisheries, the fin
is the only part of the shark which is used. The mutilated body is dumped back overboard
(sometimes still alive) to leave space on the boat for more fins. The fins are dried
and shipped to the Orient to make high-priced soup.*

sustainable fisheries, but also because of the loss of earnings from divers coming to see sharks. Worldwide, shark-watching has become a multi-million dollar business.

Why do shark populations collapse so quickly when people begin fishing them? The answer lies in the life history of these animals. In many aspects, sharks are more similar to mammals such as whales, dolphins, or ourselves, than to other fish. Whereas most fish reach maturity in only a few years and produce thousands or millions of eggs per year, sharks take many years to reach maturity. Some species may not begin to reproduce until they are over 15 years old. Some species produce as few as two pups biannually, averaging only one offspring per year. So when a population is overfished, it may take many years to recover, or it may never recover. Some scientists believe that sharks should never be fished at all, that their biology is too fragile to withstand any exploitation. Perhaps sharks should have the total protection given to marine mammals in many countries. Unfortunately, sharks do not have big 'fan clubs' as dolphins do.

Although both are large predators with slow reproductive rates, sharks are handicapped, from a public relations perspective, by the fact that their mouths appear to be frowning, and that they must open their mouths to pass water over their gills, exposing their teeth. Dolphins, on the other hand, always appear to be smiling, because of the shape of their mouths. Since they breathe through the blowholes on top of their heads, they do not have to open their mouths and expose their formidable teeth in order to get oxygen. But even the dolphin's smile may not protect it from the greed inspired by the high prices being offered by international buyers of shark fins. In a number of countries, fishermen are slaughtering dolphins to chop up for shark bait.

Sand tiger (or grey nurse) sharks are ferocious-looking, but feed on fish and are harmless to humans unless provoked. This specimen, unfortunately, has fishing weights caught on its gills.

The Perfect Body

What exactly is a shark? Simply put, a shark is a fish with a skeleton made primarily of flexible cartilage, not hard bone. This flexibility makes it quite easy for a shark to put its head back around by its tail — much to the chagrin of those who pull them. Minerals deposited into the teeth and backbones make these parts much harder than the rest of the skeleton and fossilized teeth provide our only record of some extinct sharks.

For purposes of scientific classification, all animals are placed into large categories called phyla (singular, phylum), which are divided into the smaller categories of class, order, family, genus, and species. The genus and species comprise the scientific name of an organism (e.g. *Carcharodon carcharias* describes the great white shark). Because of the presence of a spinal chord, sharks are placed in the phylum Chordata, along with mammals, reptiles, and other vertebrates. The class Chondrichthyes includes all animals with skeletons of cartilage: sharks, rays, and the odd rattail fish, or chimaeras. Sharks and rays collectively are called elasmobranchs. There are eight orders of sharks: **Squatiniformes**; Angel sharks. Flattened, ray-like body with the mouth at the front. No anal fin. **Pristiophoriformes**; Sawsharks. Elongated saw-like snout with long barbels. Mouth on underside. No anal fin. **Squaliformes**; Dogfish sharks. No anal fin. Two dorsal fins, often with spines. Cylindrical bodies, long snouts, and short mouths. **Hexanchiformes**; Sixgill, sevengill, and frilled sharks. Anal fin present. One dorsal fin. Six or seven gill slits. **Carcharhiniformes**; Groundsharks (including hammerhead and requiem sharks). Anal fin present. Two dorsal fins without spines. Five gill slits. Mouth behind front of eyes. Nictitating eyelid and spiral intestinal valve. **Lamniformes**; Mackerel and goblin sharks. Anal fin present. Two dorsal fins without spines. Five gill slits. Mouth behind front of eyes. No nictitating eyelid. Ring intestinal valve. **Orectilobiformes**; Carpet, nurse, and whale sharks. Anal fin present. Two dorsal fins without spines. Five gill slits. Mouth well in front of eyes. Barbels at inside edges of nostrils. **Heterodontiformes**; Bullhead sharks. Anal fin present. Two dorsal fins with spines. Large squarish head with crests over eyes and short pig-like snout.

Most sharks share a number of common characteristics. There are one or two dorsal fins on the back – usually two, with the first often much larger than the second. The paired pectoral, or side fins provide a planing surface, and produce lift from accelerated water flow over their curved surface. There are paired pelvic fins on the underside, often followed by a single anal fin. The large caudal, or tail fin, usually has an upper lobe which is larger than the lower lobe. Many sharks have a streamlined torpedo-like shape but there are dramatic exceptions. The angel shark is flat as an adaptation to a bottom-dwelling existence.

Young Tiger Shark

The majority of sharks have skin which feels rough if stroked from back to front – it can even cause abrasion injuries due to the unusual placoid scales that elasmobranchs have. They derive from the same embryonic tissue as the teeth, and each supports a tiny backwards-pointing tooth, or dermal denticle. Shark species have a fascinating variety of differently-shaped denticles.

Each shark species has a uniquely-shaped set of teeth, adapted for its diet. Some have flat teeth for crushing shellfish. Others have long, narrow teeth for seizing fish, or broad, serrated teeth for cutting apart larger prey or carrion. The upper teeth can be shaped differently from the lower teeth. Behind the functional row of teeth are rows of back-ups, usually folded down flat against the gums, which are brought forward and erected as the primary teeth break off or are lost. A shark may have dozens to hundreds of teeth in its mouth at once, and go through thousands in a lifetime.

The long pectoral fins of a blue shark are shaped like, and
function in the same manner as airplane wings. Water flowing over
the curved leading edge and upper surface is accelerated, creating a low pressure
which pulls the shark forward and up. This enables the shark to 'glide'
through the water with a minimal expenditure of energy.

Great white sharks are superbly evolved for their role as apex predators in temperate coastal waters. Predation, however, is a relatively rare event – sharks may go for days or weeks between meals.

Sharks' jaws are different from most other animals in that neither jaw is solidly attached to the skull – both are attached only by muscles and tendons, giving sharks the ability to sling their jaws out in front of their heads and open them very wide. It was thought that sharks had to roll over to feed at the surface because the majority have mouths on the underside of the head. Nothing could be further from the truth.

Once swallowed, the food passes through the U-shaped stomach, and digestion begins. Some species can evert the stomach out of the mouth to get rid of indigestible items such as fish bones, bird feathers, or pieces of turtle shell. Next the food passes into the short, tubular intestine where the efficiency of food utilization is improved by an absorptive membrane which increases the surface area. In the ground sharks, food winds its way through this structure, called the spiral valve, like it's going down a spiral staircase. Food passes

The lower teeth of a great white shark.

through the valve extremely slowly, taking several days. This slow digestive rate means the shark cannot feed often. Lemon sharks, one of the few species which have been studied in any detail, eat, on average, every three or four days. The idea that sharks feed constantly is a myth.

Like all fish, sharks breathe by extracting oxygen from seawater through the gills. Whereas bony fishes have a hard plate covering the gills, with a single opening, sharks have five, six, or seven gill slits for the water to flow out after passing over the gills.

Generally, the gills are aerated by opening the mouth while swimming, but some bottom-dwelling species are able to do this by using muscular contractions.

Unlike most bony fishes, sharks do not have an air bladder, a sac to which they can add or remove gas to control their buoyancy. Instead, an extremely large liver helps to keep them from sinking. The liver is full of oil (which is lighter than water) and can be as much as 25% of the body weight. However, most sharks are still heavier than water, therefore they must either swim constantly to avoid sinking, or rest on the bottom. One exception is the sand tiger shark. This shark has developed the odd habit of going to the surface to swallow air into its stomach, which then acts as an air bladder, enabling it to remain motionless without sinking. When caught on fishing lines, these sharks sometimes belch out their air supply, earning the species the nicknames 'belching' or 'roaring shark'.

The ground and requiem sharks have another unique structure called a nictitating membrane, which comes up from beneath the eye to protect it during feeding or other potentially hazardous situations. It is similar to the membranes that some birds and reptiles use for the same purpose. Other types of sharks have different protective mechanisms for the eye. Mackerel sharks, such as the great white, roll the eye up into the socket during feeding. Whale sharks are able to retract the eye back into the head when threatened, and partially cover it with a fold of skin.

Another distinctive feature of elasmobranchs is the spiracle, a hole on either side of the head behind the eyes which may be barely visible, if at all. In rays the spiracle is large and serves as an intake valve for pumping water over the gills. Bottom-dwelling sharks tend to have larger spiracles than other species, so they may use them in respiration. But in most sharks they are reduced in size, and the function, if any, is uncertain. In some species, they may serve a sensory purpose, as nerve endings line the inside. The whale shark has very large spiracles which the suckerfish accompanying them use as hiding places if threatened.

The Caribbean reef shark (opposite) is a common species in the West Indies.

The function of the oddly-shaped heads of sharks in the hammerhead family is still uncertain. It occurs in all nine members of the family Sphyrnidae.

Reproduction and Lifestyle

Sex among sharks can be a rather brutal affair. When a male senses that a female is receptive (probably by smelling chemicals that she releases into the water), he pursues her. Sometimes there can be a pack of males pursuing a single female. The male seizes his partner with the only tools available to him: his teeth. He may bite her back and flanks, inflicting considerable damage, before finally seizing her by a pectoral fin, or by the skin behind the head. In some species, the skin of the female is three times as thick as that of the male – a feature with obvious survival value.

Whereas the reproductive tract of females opens into the cloaca, a slit which also contains the urinary and anal openings, male elasmobranchs possess characteristic reproductive organs called claspers. The claspers are paired and found between the pelvic fins. A groove running down the center of each clasper directs sperm into the female's reproductive tract during sex. The term 'clasper' dates from Aristotle, and refers to his mistaken belief that the male used these organs to clasp the female. Having gained a hold on the female, the male wraps his tail around her and inserts one clasper into her cloaca. His sperm then travels up her oviduct, where it may fertilize an egg, or be stored until an egg is released at a later time. Internal fertilization, as practiced by sharks, marine mammals and marine reptiles, is rare in the ocean. Most sea creatures release their eggs into the water or attach them to the sea-bottom where they are then fertilized by the male outside the female's body. There are three strategies used by sharks for dealing with the fertilized egg: oviparity; ovoviviparity; and viviparity.

Horn sharks, swell sharks, cat sharks, and some others package the egg in an egg case, which is deposited on the ocean floor, usually attached by tendrils to an object. The developing embryo lives off the egg yolk until it is consumed, then splits open the egg case to escape. The empty egg cases often wash ashore where people find them and call them 'mermaid's purses'. Sharks which lay eggs are called oviparous. In other sharks,

Swell sharks received their name from
their ability to defend against predation by
swallowing water and swelling up to make themselves
larger. Their egg capsules are left on the ocean floor
and hatch after 7-10 months.

A baby swell shark emerges from its egg case.

including tiger sharks, nurse sharks, and makos, the eggs develop inside the shark's body, and are born live. These sharks are called ovoviviparous. In most cases the embryos live off the yolk sac only until they are born, but in some mackerel sharks and their relatives, however, once their own egg yolk is used up, the first sharks to hatch begin to feed on the other eggs and embryos. Some, such as the sand tiger, devour all of their siblings, leaving one baby shark in the uterus. 'Intrauterine cannibalism' was discovered by biologist

The sixgill shark, common in deep, cold waters.

Stewart Springer when he reached inside the body of a dead sand tiger shark he was dissecting, and was bitten on the finger by a hungry embryo.

Most of the requiem sharks and their relatives, including hammerheads and lemon sharks, reproduce by a method that is quite remarkable for a fish. In fact, it is almost identical to our own, but evolved millions of years earlier. In these sharks, the embryos are connected to a tissue called a yolk-sac placenta, which serves exactly the same function as the placenta in mammals. Animals giving true live birth by this method are said to be viviparous. Unlike mammals, however, sharks receive no further nourishment from their mothers after birth. From the moment they leave the womb, baby sharks must begin to feed on their own.

As they grow, sharks' habitat and diet, in most cases, will change. A number of species give birth in estuarine areas, where the young feed on small crabs, shrimp, and other creatures. As they grow older, they gradually move out to deeper water and become more dependent on fish and squid. Some sharks, such as horn sharks and nurse sharks, feed on shellfish throughout their lives, grinding them up with the flat plates in their mouths. Great hammerheads seem to favor stingrays, while tiger sharks are more likely to take sea turtles and sea-birds. Tiger sharks have perhaps the broadest diet of any shark, making them a danger to humans. Even more dangerous, in certain regions, is the great white shark. It specializes in marine mammals, such as sea lions, in addition to large fish like tuna. Along with the tiger shark it scavenges the carcasses of whales and other animals, and has serrated teeth useful for cutting large chunks out of prey or carrion.

One of the most unusual feeding methods is that of the cookie-cutter shark, which has a lower jaw shaped like an ice-cream scoop with serrated edges. Apparently these diminutive (40cm, or 16in) sharks use luminous organs in their mouths to attract larger animals which might prey on small luminescent squid and shrimp. The shark then lunges at the would-be predator, sinking its teeth deep into its victim's flesh, twisting around until it has removed a plug of flesh. The crater-like wounds it leaves are commonly seen on oceanic dolphins, whales and large pelagic fish. They can reside in water over 2,000m (6,500ft) deep during the day, occasionally surfacing at night, and have even attacked the floating bodies of drowned fishermen.

Because of the unpredictable availability of prey, many sharks seem to be adapted to a 'feast or famine' feeding regime, gorging themselves when they can, and then going for long periods without feeding, cruising slowly to conserve energy. Even under the best conditions, many sharks can feed only every few days because of their slow digestive rate. This is translated into a very slow growth rate. Both feeding and growth rates are much less than in most bony fish. Some sharks, notably the mako and great white, which feed on fast-swimming fish, have evolved a warm-blooded physiology which enables them to maintain an elevated metabolism, and may improve the efficiency of their muscles. By transferring heat from veins to arteries, they are able to maintain a body temperature that is higher than the surrounding sea water.

As sharks grow, the risk of predation decreases greatly, but even fully mature sharks can fall prey to orcas (killer whales), and to larger sharks. As they are born at a fairly large size (about 60cm, or 2ft for a lemon shark; 90cm, or 3ft for a sand tiger), juvenile mortality is much lower than for most marine animals. Still, there are many animals, from crocodiles to seals to other fish, which can eat them. Many sharks are not hesitant to prey on their own kind – a 2.7m (9ft) lemon shark was once found in the stomach of a 4.6m (15ft) great hammerhead.

In spite of the danger of cannibalism, some species exhibit complex social interactions, and some school in large numbers. Because of the difficulty of studying these relationships, very little is known about sharks' social systems but they have 'friendly' relations with certain other fishes, often accompanied by sharksuckers, pilot fishes, jacks (trevallies), and other fish. These eat the scraps of sharks' meals and may also help the shark find food. Sharksuckers gather on pregnant lemon sharks as they approach full term. When the pup is born, the suckerfish eat the afterbirth, and even assist by breaking, and eating, the umbilical cord. Some of the fish which accompany sharks rub their sides against the shark's rough skin, presumably to dislodge parasites. Other fish swarm over sharks and pick off the shark's parasites for an easy meal. These fish wait for the sharks at certain places on the reef called 'cleaning stations'. Sharks will coast into these stations and slow almost to a stall to enable these smaller fish to give them a 'manicure'.

While no shark is immune to predation or disease, the rate of natural mortality for large sharks is very slow. All of the other life history characteristics we have seen, from low birth rate to slow growth and delayed reproductive maturity, have evolved in conjunction with this slow rate of mortality to keep populations in balance. This balance has been seriously disrupted by new, high levels of fishing pressure, with catastrophic results for shark populations, and probably serious consequences for other forms of ocean life.

The megamouth shark species (opposite) was only discovered in 1976.

Sand tigers are known as ragged tooth sharks in South Africa and as grey nurse sharks in Australia.
They are most active at night and rest at day.

Super Senses

In order to find their prey, avoid their enemies, and deal with the many other problems of life in the marine environment, sharks have evolved a superb array of sensory capabilities. It was once believed that sharks had very poor vision and could not see colors. It is now known that only a very few species lack this ability. However, since most of the light in the ocean is concentrated in the blue-green end of the spectrum, sharks' eyes are most sensitive to these colors. They are also extremely sensitive in low light. Both these adaptations stem from a high concentration of rod cells in the retina, and to a reflective layer, called the tapetum, which effectively doubles the amount of light reaching the retina. Due to this capacity they can probably hunt by starlight. While their vision appears to be quite sharp, measurements of their eyes indicate that they may be far-sighted. If so, it is not a serious handicap, as other senses become more important at close range.

Sharks share with bony fishes a system of sensory pits known as the lateral line system. The zone of highest sensitivity is along a line stretching the length of the body on each side of the fish. These pits contain nerve endings which are highly sensitive to vibrations in the water. They can detect sounds within our hearing range, but also low-frequency vibrations such as those produced by struggling or wounded fish. The inner ears contain semicircular canals which are probably used in balance and motion detection, as well as vibration sensors that work in connection with the lateral line system. The inner ear opens to the outside through a tiny hole on the upper surface of the head — so small that it is hardly noticeable.

Sharks have been called 'swimming noses'. This is one popular conception which for most species is accurate. Some sharks have demonstrated the ability to detect chemicals in the water at concentrations as low as one part per million. By swinging their heads from side to side, and sampling the water with the nostril on either side,

The flattened body of the angel shark illustrates the great diversity
in both form and habits among sharks. The angel shark spends most of its
time lying motionless on the sea-bottom, often buried or partially buried by sand
or mud, waiting to ambush the fish and invertebrates that it feeds on.

or by swimming in a zigzag pattern, sharks can follow a scent trail for miles. They probably use scents to communicate among each other, for example to signal sexual receptivity. Although most sharks' nostrils are not connected to the respiratory system, in some bottom-dwelling sharks, such as nurse sharks, there is a connection which draws water through the nostrils when the shark pumps water across its gills. Thus it can sample the water for interesting scents even when it is not swimming.

Like other animals, sharks have taste buds in their mouths, but only certain groups of sharks have tongues. At the base of the dermal denticle on each placoid scale, there is a sensory pit with a nerve ending. It was previously believed that these were taste buds, enabling the shark to sample potential prey by rubbing against it. However, this has been proven untrue – the pits are probably water pressure sensors. There are also stretch receptors in the skin which alert sharks to pressure waves, such as those created by swimming fish.

Lemon Shark

Perhaps the most interesting adaptation found in elasmobranchs is the electromagnetic sense. Sensory pores known as *ampullae of Lorenzini* are concentrated around the snouts of sharks. These organs are capable of detecting electric fields as weak as 0.01 microvolts per cm (0.004 microvolts per in), equivalent to one AA battery with the terminals 1.5 km (almost a mile) apart. An electric field is created when charged particles move through a magnetic field. Since a shark's body is full of ions, which are charged particles, it creates an electric field as it moves through the earth's magnetic field. By sensing this field it can determine the strength and direction of the magnetic field through which it is passing. It has been shown experimentally that sharks and rays use this ability for navigation. Seawater also contains many charged particles (mostly salt ions), so ocean currents flowing through the earth's magnetic field also create electric fields. Sharks can probably sense these to obtain information about water movements around them. More importantly, the bioelectric activity which triggers muscle contractions, such as a heartbeat, also creates an electric field. By sensing these fields, sharks can home in on prey, even with their eyes covered for protection, or when the prey is hidden. Sometimes hammerheads use their flattened heads like metal detectors, sweeping them back and forth over the sand searching for stingrays or other buried fish.

When tracking prey, different senses may be used at different stages in the hunt. At great distances, a shark may be alerted to the presence of a wounded fish by detecting the vibrations of its spasmodic swimming. Approaching closer, perhaps still hundreds of meters away, it may pick up the scent trail of its leaking body fluids. Following the scent line into visual range, within tens of meters, it could use eyesight to identify the prey and start the final approach. At the last moment of the attack, a meter (a few feet) or less away, the eyes are covered or rolled back, and the electric sense takes precedence as the prey is seized. This explains why sharks attracted to boats with bait often turn and bite some metallic object at the last moment. The corrosion of metal in seawater creates an electric field stronger than any around the dead bait fish. It also explains why sharks may continue to attack their original victim, even when the victim is surrounded by a number of rescuers – a stronger bioelectric field is formed anywhere the skin is broken.

Blue sharks (opposite) are bold, but not normally aggressive to humans.

Shark Gallery

Whale Shark

Whale sharks are the largest fish in the world, and one of the most mysterious. They are generally harmless to humans, although there have been injuries due to boats colliding with whale sharks feeding at the surface, and to swimmers who got in the way of the huge tail. They are sometimes curious about humans, but more often are indifferent or avoid them.

Whale sharks feed by filtering plankton from the water as they swim, but also feed more actively, sucking in schooling fishes such as sardines and anchovies, and even take in fish as large as tuna. They have been observed feeding in a vertical, head-up position, rising slowly up and down while swallowing schooling fish, which may be trying to escape tuna or other predators, or in pursuit of smaller fish. A 36cm (14in) whale shark embryo was found in an egg case that was dredged up from the bottom of the Gulf of Mexico, but it is suspected that this was probably ejected prematurely, and that the eggs are normally retained within the female and born live. The smallest free-swimming one ever seen was 55cm (22in) long and had an umbilical scar, so they may be born at about this size. Apparently they spend their lives roaming the world's oceans, following seasonal concentrations of food organisms. Dozens appear annually off Ningaloo Reef in Australia following the coral spawn there, mostly immature males. Their size, broad, flat head with the mouth at the very front, and spotted color pattern make this shark unmistakable. The question of why such a large fish needs to camouflage itself with spots is another interesting puzzle. Unexplained scars on some individuals suggest that they may be subject to attack by sharks and/or orcas.

Order: Orectolobiformes

Family: Rhincodontidae (Rhiniodontidae), *Rhincodon (Rhiniodon) typus*

Maximum length: uncertain; measured over 12m (about 40ft), but may reach over 18m (about 60ft)

Reproduction: unknown; suspected ovoviviparous

Distribution: circumglobal; tropical and warm temperate oceans; coastal, insular, and oceanic

Diet: small to medium-sized fishes, squid, and planktonic crustaceans

Tiger Shark

Tiger sharks are born at a size of 50-76cm (20-30in) with a beautiful silvery pattern of leopard-like spots, which change to bars as the animal grows, then fade as it matures. Large individuals tend to have a simple color scheme of dark above and light below. The head is large and blocky with big, soulful eyes. The young are delicately slender, while older specimens become very stout. Tiger sharks may be found in both shallow coastal waters and deep oceanic waters. They may be resident in certain areas for undefined periods, but in general they are wanderers. Tag returns indicate movements as great as 3,193km (1,984 miles). Tiger sharks grow and mature slowly, and do not reach reproductive maturity until they have attained a size of 2.7m (9ft) or larger.

They are extremely generalized feeders, and take a large variety of items, living, dead, and inanimate. The distinctive scalloped and serrated teeth are useful for sawing through sea turtle shells and whale carcasses. They also take large numbers of sharks, rays, sea-birds and sea snakes, as well as a wide variety of fish, shellfish, seals, dolphins, and terrestrial animals (including pigs, horses, and cattle) which enter, or are washed into, the sea.

They tend to stay in deeper water by day, and enter shallow areas to feed at night. More than any other shark, they have suffered sensory confusion from the large amounts of debris dumped into the ocean by humans, and have been caught with a wide variety of indigestible objects in their stomachs, including kegs of nails, rolls of tarpaper, raincoats, and tennis shoes. Their non-specific feeding habits and large size make them a serious concern to humans, and there have been a number of confirmed attacks on divers, swimmers, surfers, and shipwreck victims.

Order: Carcharhiniformes

Family: Carcharhinidae, *Galeocerdo cuvier*

Maximum length: 7.4m (about 24ft)

Reproduction: ovoviviparous; litter size 10-82

Distribution: circumglobal in tropical and temperate seas; coastal, insular, and pelagic

Diet: fish; mammals; birds; reptiles; invertebrates; carrion and refuse

Sometimes known as 'swimming garbage cans',
tiger sharks are extremely generalized feeders and take a large variety
of items, living, dead, and inanimate.

Zebra Shark

Zebra sharks are also known as leopard sharks, but should not be confused with the unrelated California leopard shark (*Triakis semifasciatum*). The names come from the beautiful striped pattern of the juveniles and spotted pattern of adults. The body form is similar to the nurse shark, with the nasal barbels and elongated upper lobe of the caudal fin, but the large head, prominent lengthwise ridges, and silvery to yellow coloration are unique. Its habits are also similar to the nurse shark, resting on the bottom by day, and feeding on benthic fish and invertebrates by night. It is docile and non-aggressive towards humans.

Order: Orectolobiformes

Family: Stegostomatidae, *Stegostoma fasciatum* (*aka S. varium and S. tigrinum*)

Maximum length: 3.5m (about 11ft)

Reproduction: oviparous; 1-4 eggs laid at a time in dark cases 13-17cm x 8cm (5-7in x 3in), anchored with tufts of hair-like fibers

Distribution: tropical – warm temperate Indian and West Pacific Oceans and Red Sea; coastal and insular

Diet: primarily shellfish, but also small bony fishes

Caribbean Reef Shark

These medium-sized sharks are the most common sharks around coral reefs in the Caribbean, Florida, Bahamas, and Gulf of Mexico. They are difficult to distinguish in the field from a number of similar species, such as bull sharks and blacktips. Because of their preference for a shallow coral reef habitat, their appetite for fresh fish, and their bold disposition, they come into frequent conflict with spearfishermen, and cause a number of serious injuries and deaths each year. They are easily conditioned to accept handouts at underwater shark feeding shows. Their most unusual characteristic is their habit of taking 'naps' on the bottom, usually under ledges or in caves. When the phenomenon of 'sleeping sharks' was first discovered near Isla Mujeres, Mexico, it was believed that there was something special about a particular set of caves that attracted the sharks. Later it was found that this behavior occurs throughout the range of the species.

Order: Carcharhiniformes

Family: Carcharhinidae, *Carcharhinus perezi*

Maximum length: 2.95m (about 9ft)

Reproduction: viviparous; litter size unknown

Distribution: Western Atlantic, Caribbean, Gulf of Mexico; coastal and insular

Diet: mostly bony fishes

Why scalloped hammerheads school is uncertain, but their complex social interactions dispel the notion of sharks as simple-brained eating machines.

Scalloped Hammerhead

These are among the most dramatic of sharks, both because of their unusual appearance, and because they form schools which can number into many hundreds of individuals. The purpose of the schooling behavior is not known, but appears to occur only during the shark's daytime resting phase. It is believed that the schools break up at night when the sharks do most of their feeding. Schooling may occur primarily to facilitate social interactions, such as mating, or it may function to reduce each individual's risk of predation. Schools are composed mostly of small to medium size sharks, which are subject to predation by larger sharks such as tiger or white sharks and orcas (killer whales).

The bizarre head design occurs in all nine members of the family Sphyrnidae. Its function is uncertain. Since great hammerheads (*Sphyrna mokarran*) specialize in feeding on stingrays, it has been proposed that the broad, flat head evolved to provide a larger surface for electro-receptor detection of buried prey. Scalloped hammerheads have also been seen scanning sandy bottoms for buried prey. The head shape may also serve to position the eyes out where they are safer from the strike of a stingray's tailbarb – great hammerheads are sometimes caught with hundreds of barbs stuck in the throat area. Another theory is that the greater separation of the eyes and nostrils increases sight and smell capabilities. It may be that the head serves as a planing surface to compensate for the rather small pectoral fins, which may not provide adequate lift for the heavy body.

While great hammerheads take large prey, and may occasionally be of some concern to divers and swimmers, scalloped hammerheads are generally inoffensive and quite shy.

Order: Carcharhiniformes

Family: Sphyrnidae, *Sphyrna lewini*

Maximum length: 4.2m (about 14ft)

Reproduction: viviparous; litter size 15-31

Distribution: circumglobal in tropical and warm temperate oceans; coastal and insular

Diet: fish; squid; octopus; some crabs; shrimp; lobster; snails; smaller sharks and rays

Basking Shark

Basking sharks are the second largest fish in the sea (after whale sharks). They are even more passive than whale sharks in their feeding, swimming slowly just below the surface with mouths widely agape, filtering plankton through the gill rakers. They often feed or bask in groups. The buoyancy provided by their massive oil-filled livers keeps them afloat, but this has also been their undoing, leading to harpoon fisheries taking the sharks for their oil. Gavin Maxwell, describing the early days of an Irish fishery once wrote that, 'They were packed as tight as sardines, each barely allowing room for the next, layer upon layer of them, huge grey shapes like a herd of submerged elephants.' By the 1980s, a film-maker had to search for months to find a single basking shark to film off Ireland. Populations in other areas have suffered similar declines.

Basking sharks may be responsible for many 'sea serpent' sightings, because of their appearance while feeding, with widely-spaced fins breaking the surface. Several sharks may feed in rows, creating the illusion of an even longer 'serpent'. Their appearance is quite unusual, with the narrow extended snout, bulging cheeks, and huge mouth, through which the gill rakers can be seen while feeding. In the winter, when the plankton they feed on is scarce, they shed their gill rakers and become very rare in surface waters. It has been speculated that they go to the bottom and hibernate until spring.

Most of their life history is still a mystery. They are non-aggressive to humans (unless harpooned), but have long dermal denticles, pointing forward and sideways, as well as back, which can cause lacerations if contact is made with the skin.

Order: Lamniformes

Family: Cetorhinidae, *Cetorhinus maximus*

Reproduction: presumed ovoviviparous

Maximum length: 10-15m (about 32-50ft)

Distribution: worldwide in temperate oceans; coastal

Diet: plankton, including small crustaceans and eggs and larvae of crabs and fishes

Basking sharks are sometimes found floating at sea, or washed up on a beach. Their oddly-shaped bodies may have been mistaken in the past for sea serpents or other fanciful creatures.

Blue Shark

Many consider this species the most beautiful of all sharks, with their large eyes, velvety blue skin and sleek contours. The perfect streamlining and large wing-like pectoral fins are a requirement for endlessly cruising the open ocean. Tagged blues have been recaptured over 2,324 km (1,444 miles) from the point of release. They can bear over 100 pups at a time and this high reproductive rate helps to compensate for the lack of shelter for the small sharks in the open ocean. It may not be sufficient, however, to replace the countless thousands killed in drift nets.

In temperate waters, blue sharks swim near the surface, but in tropical seas are most likely to be found in deeper, cooler water. They are bold but normally non-aggressive unless stimulated by blood or fish juices in the water.

Order: Carcharhiniformes

Family: Carcharhinidae, *Prionace glauca*

Maximum length: 3.8m (about 12ft)

Reproduction: viviparous; litter size 4-135

Distribution: circumglobal; oceanic

Diet: small fish and squid; occasional pelagic crabs and shrimp, seabirds, sharks, and carrion

Port Jackson Shark

Like all horn or 'bullhead' sharks, the Port Jackson shark has a large, square head, and a sharp spine, or horn, at the front of each of the dorsal fins, which is erected to deter predators. Their color pattern also camouflages them well as they rest motionless in caves or gullies. They are able to pump water in the first gill slit and out the last four for respiration, without opening the mouth. They are active by night, picking prey off the sea-bottom, or 'vacuuming' it out of the sand, and grinding it up with the flat tooth-plates. They are non-aggressive towards humans. The large, spiral egg cases are laid at specific nest sites each year. Seven similar species in the genus *Heterodontus* are found in various parts of the Pacific and Indian Oceans.

Order: Heterodontiformes

Family: Heterodontidae *Heterodontus portusjacksoni*

Maximum length: 1.65m (about 5ft)

Reproduction: oviparous; egg cases 13-17cm x 5-7cm (5-7in x 2-3in), laid two at a time, 10-16 per season

Distribution: south, east, and west Australia; coastal

Diet: benthic invertebrates, including sea urchins, sea stars, worms, snails, prawns crabs, and barnacles; some small fish

The shape and size of sharks' teeth vary greatly according to the feeding habits of the particular species. The great white has large, serrated, triangular teeth ideally suited for sawing chunks out of large prey.

Great White Shark

White sharks, or white pointers, are the largest predatory fish in the ocean, and the only one which prey regularly on marine mammals, as well as on large fish such as tuna. Attacks on humans may result from confusion with sea lions, which are among their regular prey items. The white is not above consuming humans, but most often bite only once and release the victim without consuming any of it. Two explanations have been offered. One is that the shark doesn't like the taste of human flesh (or neoprene wet-suits). The other explanation is that white sharks have adopted a 'bite and release' strategy to let their prey bleed to death before eating it, to avoid being injured by the struggling prey.

Apart from the fact that they occasionally bite people, we know almost nothing about these awesome predators. The name is misleading, as only the underside is white, to make the shark less visible when viewed from beneath against the light surface. The back is dark, like most fish, to make it less visible when viewed from above against the dark bottom. Whites are distinguished by their great size, cone-shaped snout, large triangular teeth, and black, expressionless eyes, similar to those of the mako. Like makos, they maintain a body temperature higher than the water they swim in.

White sharks are not highly valued as food for human consumption, but the jaws can be sold for huge profits. Their numbers appear to have been significantly reduced by trophy hunting and sport-fishing. As a result, they have been declared a protected species in some areas, including South Africa and California.

Order: Lamniformes

Family: Lamnidae, *Carcharodon carcharias*

Maximum length: At least 6.4m, possibly over 8m (about 21-26ft)

Reproduction: presumed ovoviviparous; litter size up to at least nine

Distribution: worldwide; mostly in temperate waters; coastal

Diet: bony fish; sharks; rays; marine mammals; carrion; occasionally birds, turtles, and garbage

The sand tiger shark has developed the odd habit of going
to the surface to swallow air into its stomach, which then acts as an
air bladder, enabling it to remain motionless without sinking. When caught on
fishing lines, these sharks sometimes belch out their air supply, earning
the species the nicknames 'belching' or 'roaring shark'.

Sand Tiger / Grey Nurse / Ragged Tooth

The toothy 'grins' of sand tigers give them a ferocious appearance, and they do feed voraciously upon small fishes by night (and occasionally by day), but they are extremely docile in their normal daytime resting mode. Groups of a few to dozens of individuals hover in caves, gullies, and around shipwrecks, where they can be approached by skin and scuba divers with relative ease, making them ideal subjects for underwater shark-watching tours. During the 1960s whole populations were wiped out by divers with explosive speartips, who slaughtered the harmless sharks in order to look like heroes risking death to slay 'man-eaters'. They have also suffered from over-collecting for oceanaria, fishing for vitamin A, and most recently, longlining for flesh and for soupfins. Females are easily killed off, as they tend to be resident at specific sites, while males migrate more often. In Australia, they are known as 'grey nurse sharks', although they are unrelated to the true nurse sharks. In South Africa they are known as 'ragged tooth sharks'. In Australia, a number of grey nurse attacks on human beings have been reported, but this is apparently due to confusion with other types of sharks.

Sand tigers are unusual in their ability to swallow air in order to achieve neutral buoyancy, allowing them to maintain position in the water without swimming. They are also unique in their social nature. They have been observed to feed cooperatively. Adults have a distinctive appearance, with a high 'hunched' back, narrow snout with protruding awl-like teeth, and a golden-brown sheen to the skin, which may have large spots. The related smalltooth sand tiger (*Odontaspis ferox*) and bigeye sand tiger (*Odontaspis noronhai*) are found in deeper water.

Order: Lamniformes
Family: Odontaspididae, *Carcharias taurus*
Maximum length: 3.2m (about 11ft)
Reproduction: ovoviviparous with intrauterine cannibalism; litter size 2
Distribution: east coast of North America; SE coast of South America; Mediterranean; NW and SE coasts of Africa; Red Sea; SE Asia; and Australia; coastal
Diet: bony fishes; small sharks; rays; squid; crabs and lobster

Megamouth

Megamouth sharks were unknown until 1976 when one got its teeth caught on a pair of parachutes being used as sea anchors by a US Navy research vessel. The species is the only known representative of its family, and is still only known from six specimens. One was caught alive off California, and was subsequently released with a transmitting tag which enabled scientists to track it for two days. Megamouths have large flabby bodies, and tiny hooked teeth. They stay in water hundreds of feet deep by day but migrate up to water as shallow as 20m (65ft) at night, probably following the migrations of the shrimp they feed on. They apparently feed by swimming slowly with the mouth open and filtering the shrimp out of the water, but the silvery lining of the mouth, and what appear to be luminescent organs suggest that they may also use light to lure their prey into their huge, gaping mouths.

Order: Lamniformes

Family: Megachasmidae, *Megachasma pelagios*

Maximum length: unknown; at least 5.2m (at least 17ft)

Reproduction: unknown

Distribution: known from Pacific and Indian Oceans; probably worldwide

Diet: small shrimps and jellyfish

Spotted Wobbegong

Wobbegongs are also known as carpet sharks, an appropriate name related to their habit of lying on the sea-bottom like a rug, and to their flattened, frilly, well-camouflaged appearance. The camouflage may enable them to feed by day, using a 'lurk and lunge' strategy. Prey may even nibble on its fringe of lip flaps before being gulped down. They probably feed by night, when they are more active. Upper and lower fang-like teeth mesh to trap or impale prey. These can cause severe injuries to humans who step on or otherwise provoke a wobbegong, but they are normally non-aggressive. The light O-shaped spots distinguish the spotted wobbegong from the similar tasselled wobbegong, Japanese wobbegong, ornate wobbegong, and northern wobbegong. The tasselled wobbegong, *Eucrossorhinus dasypogon*, has skin flaps on both the upper and lower jaws, while the others have frills on only the upper jaw.

Order: Orectolobiformes

Family: Orectolobidae, *Orectolobus maculatus*

Maximum length: 3.2m (about 10ft)

Reproduction: ovoviviparous; litter size up to 37

Distribution: Australia; Japan; South China Sea; coastal

Diet: crabs, lobsters, octopus; other benthic invertebrates and bony fishes

*Makos must be regarded as potentially dangerous due to
their aggressive temperament, rapid swimming, and capacity for consuming
large prey. Makos are highly valued both as food fish and as sport fish. Important
commercial fisheries occur in California, the Mediterranean, West Africa,
the Gulf of Mexico, and the Caribbean.*

Shortfin Mako

Mako sharks are the speed kings of the cartilaginous fish, and possibly the fastest fish in the ocean. No reliable method has been devised to obtain an accurate speed reading for them, but measurements as high as 97kph (60mph) have been reported. When hooked by anglers they may jump to a height of several body lengths out of the water. They are able to chase down and consume such fast-moving pelagics as tunas, mackerel, and swordfish. Their ability to reach such phenomenal speeds may be partly attributed to a blood vessel heat exchange system which enables them to maintain a body temperature higher than the surrounding seawater. Few attacks on humans have been recorded, possibly because the offshore habitat they prefer makes contact with swimmers infrequent.

Makos are torpedo-shaped in appearance, with a metallic blue back, light underside and a lateral keel on either side of the tail. The solid black eye is similar to that of white sharks, while the narrow protruding teeth are like those of the sand tiger. The teeth develop broader cusps as the animal ages. This is thought to correspond with a change in diet from small fish which are taken whole, to one which includes larger prey, which must be cut up before consumption.

While primarily oceanic, where they have been found from the surface to a depth of over 150m (500ft), shortfin makos are sometimes seen near reef drop-offs and kelp beds. The dorsal fins are frequently 'decorated' with thread-like parasitic copepods. The similar longfin mako (*Isurus paucus*) is less commonly seen than the shortfin, as it lives in deeper water.

Order: Lamniformes

Family: Lamnidae, *Isurus oxyrinchus*

Maximum length: 4m (about 13ft)

Reproduction: ovoviviparous; litter size 4-20

Distribution: circumglobal tropical and temperate; coastal and oceanic

Diet: primarily bony fish and other sharks; occasionally turtles, dolphins, and squid

Whitetip Reef Shark

Whitetip reef sharks are among the most common sharks found in shallow water in the Pacific and Indian Oceans. They are readily recognized by their flat squarish head with prominent nasal flaps, white tips on the dorsal fins and caudal fin, large second dorsal, and their habit of lying on the sea-bottom. They are sometimes confused with silvertip and oceanic whitetip sharks, but these prefer deeper water and never rest on the bottom. Both silvertips and oceanic whitetips are stouter and more torpedo-shaped than whitetip reefs and have a smaller second dorsal. Silvertips have white tips on all fins. Oceanic whitetips have white tips on the first dorsal, pectoral, caudal and pelvic fins, and have a large, rounded, oar-like first dorsal, and extremely long pectoral fins. Oceanic whitetips feed on turtles, birds, and the carcasses of whales and dolphins, as well as fish, and are considered much more dangerous to humans than whitetip reef sharks. Both silvertips and oceanic whitetips are much less frequently seen by divers and swimmers than whitetip reef sharks.

Whitetip reef sharks are most active at night, spending much of their day lounging around under crevices or in caves, occasionally in large groups. Sometimes small goby fish are seen cleaning parasites off their skin while the sharks are resting. While they can be roused by a wounded fish at any time, whitetips prefer to hunt by night when many reef fish are asleep in holes in the coral. Abandoning their sluggish daytime personalities, they become relentless predators and scavengers, sometimes breaking apart coral heads to get at their prey. Normally non-aggressive towards humans, they can, like any animal, become dangerous if attacked or sufficiently agitated.

Order: Carcharhiniformes

Family: Carcharhinidae, *Triaenodon obesus*

Maximum length: 2.1m (about 7ft)

Reproduction: viviparous; litter size 1-5

Distribution: wide-ranging in the tropical Indo-Pacific; coastal and insular

Diet: bony fishes; octopus; crab and lobster

Whitetip Reef Shark

Oceanic Whitetip   Silvertip Shark

Lemon Shark

Lemon sharks have two nearly equal-sized dorsal fins and a yellow cast to the skin. The narrow teeth are adapted to seizing fish, but are capable of inflicting serious damage if the shark is provoked. Lemon sharks sometimes rest on the sea-bottom, resulting in occasional injuries to waders that step on them, but are normally non-aggressive. They spend their first two years in shallow bays and lagoons, hiding in the vegetation along the shoreline. They tolerate the brackish water of these estuaries, and even enter fresh water at times. As they grow, they gradually wander seaward, ranging over coastal sand flats at around age 3-5, then tend to move out to deeper reefs as they reach adulthood. The closely related sicklefin lemon shark, *Negaprion acutidens*, is found in the central and western Pacific Ocean, Indian Ocean and Red Sea.

Order: Carcharhiniformes

Family: Carcharhinidae, *Negaprion brevirostris*

Maximum length: 3.4m (about 11ft)

Reproduction: viviparous; litter size 4-17

Distribution: east and west coasts of North and South America, west coast of Africa; coastal and insular

Diet: mostly bony fish; also octopus, crabs, shrimp and rays

Silky Shark

Silkies are slender sharks with the 'classic' requiem shark appearance, and are often confused with similar sharks. The most distinctive field mark is the extremely elongated rear margin of the second dorsal fin. Silkies tend to come closer to shore than blues or oceanic whitetips, and may be encountered by divers near oceanic islands, although casual snorkelers and swimmers are unlikely to ever see one. They can be found feeding in groups on schools of small fish, along with seabirds and tunas, and may gather under floating logs or other objects. In the Bahamas they can be found regularly around a large buoy, used for naval exercises, which is tethered in 5,000ft of water. They are curious sharks and will approach and sometimes follow divers, but have not been known to attack except when fed by humans. Dive guides in the Bahamas handle them regularly to remove fish hooks. (This is not recommended for amateurs!)

Order: Carcharhiniformes

Family: Carcharhinidae, *Carcharhinus falciformis*

Maximum length: 3.3m (about 11ft)

Reproduction: viviparous; litter size 2-14

Distribution: circumtropical; oceanic and coastal

Diet: fish

Bull sharks are often captured live for display in oceanaria, as this is one of the few species of shark which survives well in captivity.

Bull Shark

Bull sharks have confounded scientists by thriving in both fresh and seawater, and even tolerating water much saltier than seawater. Their ability to move freely between habitats of varying salinities is an astounding physiological feat. In fresh water, they are known by various names such as Zambezi shark and Lake Nicaragua shark, and are found as far as 3,700km (2,300 miles) from the sea. Like tiger sharks, their non-specialized feeding habits and large serrated teeth make them a danger to humans, the more so because they live in lakes, rivers and estuaries which puts them into close proximity with human activities. Bull sharks are credited with many attacks on humans, however, the species identification is suspect in many of these cases because of their similar appearance to a number of other requiem sharks. On the other hand, it is possible that bull sharks committed some of the attacks which inspired the novel *Jaws*, as these occurred in rivers. Reports of 'sleeping' bull sharks are also suspect, as these may well be Caribbean reef sharks, which are very similar in appearance and are known to behave this way.

Bull sharks come into coastal estuaries to pup, making populations vulnerable to disturbance from coastal development. Off Florida, schools of hundreds of females have been seen over deep reefs during the spring pupping season, but the function of these schools is not known. They are easily confused with similar sharks, but are distinguished by their stout body, short snout, small eyes, curved and pointed dorsal, and lack of distinct markings on the underside of the pectoral fins. Bull sharks are fished both commercially (for meat, soupfins, leather and oil) and for sport. Large numbers are killed in shark mesh nets protecting beaches in South Africa.

Order: Carcharhiniformes

Family: Carcharhinidae, *Carcharhinus leucas*

Maximum length: 3.4m (about 11ft)

Reproduction: viviparous; litter size 1-13

Distribution: widespread in tropical and subtropical oceans; coastal and insular; also in rivers and lakes

Diet: sharks; rays; bony fish; crabs; shrimps; squid; snails; turtles; birds; and mammals

Nurse Shark

Nurse sharks are among the most common sharks encountered on reefs of the Atlantic, Caribbean, and Gulf of Mexico. They are easily recognized by their distinctive flat heads, beady eyes, barbels, second dorsal fins nearly as large as the first, and caudal fins with an elongated upper lobe and almost no lower lobe. They are typically found resting in a cave or under a ledge, sometimes with the body or tail exposed. By night they become tenacious predators, even breaking apart coral heads to get at sleeping or wounded fish and benthic invertebrates, which they vacuum up with the powerful suction-feeding technique. The name 'nurse shark' may have its origin in observations of sharks sucking noisily on fishermen's baits, like nursing babies. The fleshy barbels (whiskers) projecting downward from the nostrils are used to test the bottom for scents of hidden prey. Their numerous short teeth are suited for crushing shellfish, but are sharp enough to cause a painful injury to the foolish person who tries to tease one. Skindivers have been known to return to the boat or the beach with a nurse shark still attached to an arm or leg (or, in one case, a breast) after grabbing one in a test of bravado.

Eggs normally hatch inside the mother's body, and the young are born alive. Sometimes egg cases are prematurely ejected, and have been found on the sea-bottom, leading to confusion about the reproductive pattern of this species. Young nurse sharks are light with dark spots and are valued as aquarium fish. Older sharks have a deep golden-brown skin with diamond-shaped dark and light flecks, which is highly prized for leather. The similar tawny nurse shark (*Nebrius ferrugineus*) is widespread in the central and western Pacific Ocean, Indian Ocean and Red Sea, while the short-tailed nurse shark (*Ginglymostoma brevicaudatum*) is restricted to the western Indian Ocean.

Order: Orectolobiformes

Family: Ginglymostomatidae, *Ginglymostoma cirratum*

Maximum length: 3-4m (about 10-13ft)

Reproduction: ovoviviparous; litter up to 28

Distribution: tropical/subtropical western and eastern Atlantic and eastern Pacific; coastal and insular

Diet: bottom-dwelling fish and invertebrates such as spiny lobster, shrimp, crabs, snails, octopus and squid

Nurse sharks are most active by night. They rely primarily on olfactory, rather than visual cues to find their prey, so they do not need daylight for hunting.

The Predator's Pedigree
Setting the (Fossil) Record Straight

The frequent statement that sharks are 'living fossils – unchanged over 400 million years', is just as inaccurate and absurd as the line that, 'all they do is eat and make baby sharks.' Sharks and bony fishes both evolved from primitive jawless fishes. The first sharks appear in the fossil record about 400 million years ago, a little later than the early bony fishes, but they are nothing like modern sharks. Most modern families of sharks appeared between about 200 million years ago, about the same time as the first mammals, and 65 million years ago, when marine mammals were colonizing the seas. The word 'primitive' is no more applicable to living sharks than it is to dolphins. Hammerheads, often cited as being primitive in appearance, are actually one of the most modern groups of sharks. The first members of this family appear in the fossil record about 24 million years ago, well into the *Cenozoic* or modern era. The study of evolution of sharks is complicated by the fact that, lacking bony skeletons, often the only parts that are preserved are the teeth. However, it is certain that sharks are continuing to evolve, as all creatures must, to meet the needs of a changing environment. Whether they can evolve fast enough to survive the pressures that mankind is putting on them is another story.

Recommended Reading

Compagno, Leonard J. V., FAO Species Catalogue, Vol. 4, *Sharks of the World*, United Nations Development Program, FAO, 1984

Gruber, Samuel H. (ed. American Littoral Society), *Discovering Sharks*, Highlands, New Jersey, 1990

Michael, Scott W., *Reef Sharks and Rays of the World*, Sea Challengers, Monterey, California, 1993

Springer, Victor and Gold, Joy, *Sharks in Question*, Smithsonian Institution Press, Washington D.C., London, 1989

Stevens, John D., ed., *Sharks*, Facts on File Publications, New York, Oxford

Biographical Notes

Doug Perrine was born in Dallas, Texas and has lived in Hawaii, North Africa and Micronesia. He currently resides in Miami, Florida, where he works as a freelance photojournalist, tour leader, and marine life consultant for motion picture projects. Sharks have fascinated him since his first encounter on a scuba dive, over twenty years ago. He holds a master's degree in marine biology from the University of Miami, and has participated in a number of shark research cruises. He also organizes oceanic adventure tours, specializing in encounters with sharks and other large marine animals. His articles and photographs appear in hundreds of magazines around the world.